Other Best Joke Books for Kids

Volume 1

Volume 2

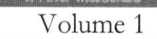
Volume 3

Volume 4

PETER MACDONALD

Best Brain Teasers For Kids-

WHO AM I ?

Peter MacDonald

Copyright © 2015 Peter MacDonald

All rights reserved.

ISBN-13:
978-1514801970

ISBN-10:
1514801973

BEST JOKE BOOKS FOR KIDS
VOLUME 5

LETS HAVE SOME MORE FUN

CONTENTS

Table of Contents

Best Brain Teasers for Kids.............................3

Benefits of Brain Teasers................................3

Easy Brain Teasers...5

Moderately Hard Brain Teasers 11

Difficult Brain Teasers 22

Brain Teaser Answer Key:..............................27

Easy Brain Teaser Answers:...........................28

Moderately Hard Brain Teaser Answers:....28

Difficult Brain Teaser Answers:.....................35

PETER MACDONALD

Best Brain Teasers for Kids

Brain teasers are word puzzles that may be spoken or written and they require you to use mental reasoning to find the answer to the puzzle. Generally, you only need your brain to solve these puzzles.

"Who Am I" puzzles challenge the reader to thing laterally and logically, developing problem solving skills.

Basically, using brain teasers is like doing a workout specifically for your brain. The more you work your brain, the stronger and more developed it becomes.

Benefits of Brain Teasers

Brain teasers offer a number of benefits, especially for children. Studies show that playing mind games, such as brain teasers, can increase blood flow to the brain, increasing the performance of the brain. The increase in blood flow also results in important chemical changes that result in improved brain function.

Using brain teasers regularly offers a fun way that children can improve cognitive skills, such as comprehension, memory, attention, perception, language skills and more. Brain teasers help to improve alertness and concentration in children. They help to activate the thinking process, exercising and stimulating the mind.

Since brain teasers are fun and exciting, children can have a great time while exercising their brain and developing improved mental skills. Brain teasers are fun to do alone, or they can be done as a team to encouraging working together. Some children even enjoy competing against friends to see who is able to figure out the right answer first.

Easy Brain Teasers

Starting out with easy brain teasers is a great way to begin getting your brain in shape. Easy brain teasers help warm up the brain, training your brain and making it stronger. Start working on these simple brain teasers before you move on to harder ones. Once you find it easy to solve the easy brain teasers, then you can go on to moderately hard teasers, working your way up to difficult ones.

Easy "Who am I" Brain Teasers

1 – You can write me forward, backward, or even upside down, yet I still can be read from left to right. Who am I?

2 – I can be cracked, I can be made. I can be told, and I can be played. Who am I?

3 – I can be long or short and I am a tool. You can use me to survive, but whether I am

good or evil depends upon the way that you use me. Who am I?

4 – I am my mother's child, my father's child, yet no one's son. Who am I?

5 – Take away my letters, yet my name will still be the same. The letters that you take I will never reclaims, since when they are gone, my name is still the same. Who am I?

6 – While you will find me in Paris, I am not found in France, and among my siblings, I happen to be the thinnest. Who am I?

7 – I am older than the computer, and you use me all the time. Sometimes I am colorful and I have tons of fiber. Who am I?

8 – I have married many, yet I have never been married. Who am I?

9 – I am water's son, yet when I am returned to water, I will die. Who am I?

10 – I was not here yesterday, yet today I am here. Tomorrow I will not be around, but I may see you once each week. Who am I?

11 – I can be pesky and sneaky, yet when I seek the truth, I often end up in trouble. Who am I?

12 – If you say my name, I no longer exist. Who am I?

13 – Let me live, and my life will be short. However, kill me and I will stay around longer. Who am I?

14 – While I live in a little house that is filled with meat, there is no door where you can go in and eat. Who am I?

15 – People walk on me all night and day, but I never get to sleep. Who am I?

16 – I can run, yet I will never get tired. Who am I?

17 – While I can be turned up and turned low, the problem is that I cannot glow. Who am I?

18 – When I am empty, nothing will move me, but I can point the way when I am filled. Who am I?

19 – I am the one who knows all of your secrets. Who am I?

20 – I only think good things, even when bad things happen. Who am I?

21 – I live for the crowd, and I live for the laughter. If you do not laugh, I have failed. Who am I?

22 – I have a bow and arrow, and I have wings. I love my job, and at my job, hate is never spoken of. I only speak of love, and I will help you fall in love too. Who am I?

23 – I really love those peanuts, all the books say. I am becoming more endangered each and every day. I weigh nearly a ton, and I will eat a ton too. Who am I?

24 – I always play fair, and I always get dirty. A diamond is my playground. When I am nearly done, I'll run home. Who am I?

25 – I was framed. However, the person who framed me did not do anything wrong. Who am I?

26 – I am very beneficial, and many people talk about me. However, it is difficult to find me during a war. I am often found at the end of a war, and without me, the world will never survive. Who am I?

27 – While I have no wings, I fly. I do not have eyes, but I can see. Even with no arms, I can climb. I am stronger than anything and I'm responsible for the evolution of society. Who am I?

28 – My mother's name is red, and my father's name is blue. Who am I?

29 – I live in the canopy and rarely touch the ground. I move so slow and spend most of my time hanging upside down. Tree leaves are my favorite food. People often call me lazy. Who am I?

30 – When I left, I had no idea where I was going. When I arrived, I was not sure where I was. When I returned, I was not sure where I had been. Who am I?

31 – I dig out tiny holes and store silver and gold in them. I make crowns of gold and

bridges of silver. Everyone needs my help, but many people are afraid of me. Who am I?

32 – Many people try to hide, and some try to cheat me. However, you and I will someday meet. Who am I.

Moderately Hard Brain Teasers

Medium-hard "Who am I" Brain Teasers

33 – Throw me out the window and you will leave a grieving wife. Who am I?

34 – I can make you feel weak in the worst times, but I actually help keep you safe. While I may make you sweat, I will also make you cold. Both the weak and the brave know me well, but the brave have learned to act despite me. Who am I?

35 – If my neighbor makes mistakes, I will eliminate them. Who am I?

36 – I am hot and I change colors depending on my heat. While I keep eating, I am never full. Who am I?

37 – You walk on me all the time. I drink and drink, yet my thirst is never quenched. Who am I?

38 – You cannot see me, but you know I am there when I run my fingers through your hair. I can sing nearly any song. Who am I?

39 – I have thirty men, but only two women, yet it is the women that have the most power. They dress in black and white, and they often fight for hours at a time. Who am I?

40 – I am the ruler of all the shoves and I have a wife. I also have a double, and I am as skinny as a thin knife. Who am I?

41 – I am easiest to see after night has fallen and I beautifully light up the sky. When I show off my colors I will help you celebrate the 4th of July.

42 – I am neither living or dead, yet I can change faces all the time. I attract many eyes. Who am I?

43 – My dinner guests always call us even when they realize their place in my meal. I do get a little bit fed up with people. Who am I?

44 – I was born in flame and conceived in earth. While some use me with shame, others use me with mirth. When I have been tamed, I rarely miss, and men everywhere fear my cold, deadly kiss. They cloak themselves in heavy shells and chains, and they try to avoid my inevitable pain. I am a gift fit for soldiers, yet I am also owned by kings, and my beauty rivals that on an angel's wings. Who am I?

45 – I can be black as the forest or pale as sunlight. Sometimes I am long, and sometimes I am short – the choice is yours. You choose the way I look. Who am I?

46 – I am watching you, and I judge people through the year. I do not need a car, because I have my own deer. Lucky for me, I only work one day out of every year. Who am I?

47 – The blackboard and chalk are my very best friends, and you often see me in the morning until the afternoon ends. While I am really smart, some people think I'm mean, but opinions of me depend on how I am seen. Who am I?

48 – There are four houses, a blue house, a green house, a red house, and a white house. A blue man lives in the blue house, the green many lives in the green house, and the red man lives in the red house. I live in the White House. Who am I?

49 – I have a lot of teeth, but no mouth. My hands use me. I come in many sizes and colors, and you probably use me every day. Who am I?

50 – While I have an eye, I am not able to see. I have no limbs, but I am still faster and stronger than any man. Who am I?

51 – I only have one leg, yet I have three eyes. Who am I?

52 – You will find me in an orchestra. However, if a lightning bolt hit the

orchestra, I am the one who would probably be hit. Who am I?

53 – I am a seven letter word. My 1st, 2nd and 3rd letters are a spell a liquid. My 3rd, 4th, 5th, and 6th letters spell a type of pain. My 6th and 7th letters spell a place you find in a hospital. Who am I?

54 – When you look at me, I smile back at you. When you wink at me, I wink back at you. When you kiss me, I kiss you back. When you say, "I love you," I will say it back. Who am I?

55 – I am often known as a right, and some think I am a reason, but everyone wants me, especially people who are trapped. Who am I?

56 – I am black and I can cause a lot of pain. I am common in children who love to eat candy. Unfortunately, you will have to pay a lot of money to get rid of me. Who am I?

57 – I am found in evil, yet I am in holy too. While I am not in heaven, I am found in hell. You can find me in excellence, but no

in badness. I am neither friend nor foe, and you will not find me in misery or woe. While you can find me in lust, I am very noble too. Although I am not in greed, you will find me in wealth. Who am I?

58 – I can be no older than a month, yet I have existed for millions and millions of years. Some think I have a man, and others think I have cheese, yet today, I have neither. Who am I?

59 – When you take your first breath, you are introduced to me. I am a memory of things that have already passed. I remind you that nothing is permanent. While I am often heralded, you cannot touch me. I am a guardian and I will lead you through the unknown. People often say that I am short. Who am I?

60 – My father's name is blue. If you mix my name with my father's name, you will have maroon. If you mix me with my mom's name, I would only get a little lighter. If you mix my mother's name and my father's name, you will get my name. Who am I?

61 – You cannot see me and you cannot touch me, yet you can hear me. Who am I?

62 – Without me, you cannot live. While I am as light as a feather, you cannot hold me for very long. Who am I?

63 – I have fingers and thumbs, yet I have no bone, I have no scales, I have no feathers, and I even have no flesh. Who am I?

64 – I am the longest word that you will ever find in a dictionary. Who am I?

65 – I have no legs, but I can dance. I have no lungs, but I have to breathe to live. Who am I?

66 – I am only one color, yet I can be many sizes. I am stuck at the bottom, yet I can easily fly. You can see me when the sun is out, but the rain chases me away. I do no harm and I feel no pain. Who am I?

67 – I am a nut, yet I have no shell. Who am I?

68 – I am usually cheaper when I am young, and I can make you happy. As I grow older, I am more valued. Who am I?

69 – If you have me, you will want to share me with someone else. But, if you share me, you will not have me anymore. Who am I?

70 – The more you have of me, the less you will be able to see. Who am I?

71 – Once I was only owned by wealthy people, but soon, everyone had me. You cannot buy me in a bookstore and you cannot take me out of a library. Today, I am almost extinct. Who am I?

72 – If you take off my skin, you will not make me cry. However, when you take off my skin, I will make you cry. Who am I?

73 – The more I dry, the wetter I get. Who am I?

BEST BRAIN TEASERS FOR KIDS – Who Am I ?

74 – You can never eat me for breakfast and you can never eat me for dinner. Who am I?

75 – I come from an egg, and I have no legs. I have a backbone, yet I am rarely straight. I can peel like an onion, yet I still am whole. I can be very long, and I can fit in a hole. Who am I?

76 – I am a five letter word, and I am usually under you. If you take away my first letter, I will be on top of you. If you take away my first and second letters, you will find me all around you. Who am I?

77 – I have a horn and I can give you milk, but I am not a cow. Who am I?

78 – I am tall and thin. I cannot walk, yet I have a tilted head. Who am I?

79 – At dusk I will appear without being fetched. I will disappear at dawn, but I will not be stolen. I am a guide to the sailors. Who am I?

80 – I start with the letter "E" and I also end with the letter "E." However, I usually only contain a single letter. Who am I?

81 – I am little more than holes that are tied to more holes. Even though I am not stiff like a pole, I am strong as steel.

82 – With pointed fangs, I sit and wait. With a heavy force, I dole out fate. Over my bloodless victims, I proclaim my might, eternally joining in just one bite. Who am I?

83 – When I am pointing up, everything is bright. When I am pointing down, everything is dark. Who am I?

84 – I am a fountain, yet no one can drink me. I am sought after like gold, yet my color is black. Who am I?

85 – Humans can create me, yet they cannot control me. I will suck on flesh, paper, wood and more. I am more costly than anyone ever thinks I will be. Who am I?

86 – If you take a minute to stop and look, you will always see me. You can try to touch me, but you will not be able to feel me. I cannot move, but when you move

closer to me, I will always move away from you. Who am I?

87 – When you want to use me, you will throw me out. When you are done using me, you will take me in. Who am I?

88 – You can break me, but you can never touch me. Who am I?

Difficult Brain Teasers

Hard "Who am I" Brain Teasers

89 – As I age, I change stature. However, no matter how old I get, I am still important. My boss determines my importance. Once we part, I am no longer of any importance. Who am I?

90 – Some people use me to get around, but I never actually touch the ground. In some cases, I fall, yet sometimes I float. Who am I?

91 – You probably have two eyes, but I only have one. Although I have an eye, I have no eyeballs. My eye is not dangerous, yet my whole is extremely dangerous. While the air is clear where you find my eye, I cannot see. Who am I?

92 – I serve many people, depending on how healthy people are. When I am successful, most people forget about me. Who am I?

93 – Sometimes I am shaped like a banana. Sometimes I am shaped like a sphere. Sometimes you cannot see me at all. Who am I?

94 – I am seen when the sun is high, and I am also seen in the darkest of night. You will find me in a holiday song when there is lots of snow so white. I am often used in the kitchen, and you will find me in a calendar. Who am I?

95 – I have a mouth, yet I cannot drink. I have a head, but I cannot think. I have a tongue, but I do not have a lung. Sometimes I am held, and sometimes I am hung. Who am I?

96 – I am a word and I am six letters long. Sometimes I enter with a loud gong. My letters are all in order, from A to Z, and I happen to start with the letter B. Who am I?

97 – I hear a lot and I say a lot, but most people never look for me. Very few people hear me, and I often hide in plain sight. All I want to do is help, but most people want to bend me. I often show up when I am least

expected, and once I come to light, there is no place to hide from me. Who am I?

98 – I am no thicker than a finger when I fold, but I can be as thick as what I am holding when I hold. Who am I?

99 – Some people are very quick to take me, yet others must be coaxed. It is those who chose to take me who can lose or gain the most. Who am I?

100 – I am guided as I scrape along, and I leave behind a snowy, against that which I am scraping. When I am scraping, I must. Who am I?

101 – I only can exist when I am between two things. Most people know very well all the hardship that I bring. Who am I?

102 – When I am broken, I will not make a lot of noise. People always break me on purpose. Who am I?

103 – In many ways, I am proudly shown, and many like me have been sewn. I never

tear from being worn, but if I am torn, I must be burned. Who am I?

104 – I have four legs, but I cannot take a walk. While I have a head, I cannot ever talk. You will often see me at the end of the day, and if you need another one, a hefty price you will pay. Who am I?

105 – If you look in my face, you will see someone. However, if you look at my back, you will see no one. Who am I?

106 – While I am feather, I am not a bird, although I have a mobile nest. I can quickly fly, and after I fly, I will also stop and rest. Who am I?

107 – I am a slayer of your regrets, both old and new. While I am sought by many, I am found by very few. Who am I?

108 – I have a blade, and it is jaggedly cut, and I will help keep your doors shut. I go into the darkness, and I wear a ring. While one of me is quiet, if you have many we will sing. Who am I?

109 – Everyone has me. Those who have the least of me are not aware that they have me. Those who have the most of me, wish they had less of me. But, no one wants to have too little of me or none at all. Who am I?

110 – While I cannot be touched, I can be felt. I cannot be opened, but you can go into me. If you seek me, you will find me under something, yet I can move from place to place. Who am I?

111 – I can make people crazy, and I will shine on you when you retire. I can move water without even a touch, and the colors I turn can cause you ire. Who am I?

112 – I grow from the soil, and live in a scented bed. If you ignore me, I will wither. Use me to apologize or show your love, but remember I need rain from up above. Who am I?

113 – I function like a witch's brew, and I can make people do things they don't want to. At the sound of my voice, you will not have a choice. You have to do what is requested of you. Who am I?

114 – While I see much, I change but little. I am firm and powerful, and I can rip apart a mounting. Yet, the wind can move me. I am often wasted, and sometimes valued. I often stand for life and give life to others. Who am I?

115 – I can easily be given away, but few people want to take me. People who are older often give me to the young. Sometimes I am true, but I often have a sting. Who am I?

Easy Brain Teaser Answers:

1 – I am the word "Noon"

2 – I am a joke

3 – I am a weapon

4 – I am a daughter

5 – I am a mailman

6 – I am the letter "I"

7 – I am paper

8 – I am a priest

9 – I am ice

10 – I am today

11 – I am curiosity

12 – I am silence

13 – I am a candle

14 – I am a nut

15 – I am a sidewalk

16 – I am a stream

17 – I am a speaker

18 – I am a balloon

19 – I am a diary

20 – I am an optimist

21 – I am a clown

22 – I am cupid

23 – I am an elephant

24 – I am a baseball player

25 – I am a painting

26 – I am peace

27 – I am imagination

28 – I am purple

29 – I am a sloth

30 – I am Christopher Columbus

31 – I am a dentist

32 – I am death

Moderately Hard Brain Teaser Answers:

33 – I am the letter "N"

34 – I am fear

35 – I am an eraser

36 – I am fire

37 – I am soil

38 – I am the wind

39 – I am the game of Chess

40 – I am the King of Spades

41 – I am a firework

42 – I am a television

43 – I am a cannibal

44 – I am a sword

45 – I am hair

46 – I am Santa Claus

47 – I am a teacher

48 – I am the president

49 – I am a comb

50 – I am a hurricane

51 – I am a traffic signal

52 – A am the conductor

53 – I am a teacher

54 – I am your reflection in a mirror

55 – I am freedom

56 – I am a cavity

57 – I am the letter "L"

58 – I am the moon

59 – I am time

60 – I am purple

61 – I am your voice

62 – I am your breath

63 – I am a glove

64 – I am the word "Smiles" (there is a mile between each "S")

65 – I am fire

66 – I am a shadow

67 – I am a doughnut

68 – I am wine

69 – I am a secret

70 – I am darkness

71 – I am a telephone book

72 – I am an onion

73 – I am a towel

74 – I am lunch

75 – I am a snake

76 – I am a chair

77 – I am a milk truck

78 – I am the number 1

79 – I am the stars

80 – I am an envelope

81 – I am a steel chain

82 – I am a stapler

83 – I am a light switch

84 – I am oil

85 – I am a baby

86 – I am the horizon

87 – I am an anchor

88 – I am a promise

Difficult Brain Teaser Answers:

89 – I am a pencil

90 – I am a boat

91 – I am a tornado

92 – I am a doctor

93 – I am the moon

94 – I am the number "12"

95 – I am a bell

96 – am the word "Begins"

97 – I am the truth

98 – I am a sack

99 – I am risk

100 – I am chalk

101 – I am distance

102 – I am bread

103 – I am a flag

104 – I am a bed

105 – I am a mirror

106 – I am an arrow

107 – I am redemption

108 – I am a key

109 – I am age

110 – I am shade

111 – I am the moon

112 – I am a flower

113 – I am the word "please"

114 – I am a tree

115 – I am advice

BEST BRAIN TEASERS FOR KIDS – Who Am I ?

ABOUT THE AUTHOR

Peter MacDonald loves a good laugh, especially ones he can share with his children. He is committed to creating good clean fun in His series of joke books, "Best Joke Books For Kids". Peter is an Aussie with a good sense of Humor and he enjoys the good things in life, especially his church and family.

Visit our website for all the latest news at

bestjokesforkids.com

Printed in Germany
by Amazon Distribution
GmbH, Leipzig